WALKING CLOSE

WELLAND near STAMFORD

Number Five in the popular series of walking guides

<u>Contents</u>

The walks contained in this booklet make use of rights of way, national recreational paths and riverside paths in the Stamford area. There is very little walking on roads except where unavoidable. Most are on firm, good quality paths and well marked and signposted. Paths may cross fields under cultivation and some are more obscure and less well directed; the detailed instructions will guide past these points. Some of the walks are in areas popular with walkers already, others are in areas less popular and perhaps less accessible. Footpaths in Rutland are helpfully marked with conspicuous yellow topped posts making the trails a lot easier to follow.

Walked, Written and Drawn by Clive Brown

© Clive Brown 2003 - 2006

© 2nd Edition 2006 – 2022

Published by Clive Brown
ISBN 978-1-907669-05-7

PLEASE
Take care of the countryside
Your leisure is someone's livelihood

Close gates
Start no fires
Keep away from livestock and animals
Do not stray from marked paths
Take litter home
Do not damage walls, hedgerows or fences
Cross only at stiles or gates
Protect plants, trees and wildlife
Keep dogs on leads
Respect crops, machinery and rural property
Do not contaminate water

Although not essential we recommend good walking boots; during hot weather take something to drink on the way. All walks can easily be negotiated by an averagely fit person. The routes have been walked and surveyed by the author, changes can however occur, please follow any signed diversions. Some paths cross fields which are under cultivation. All distances and times are approximate.

The maps give an accurate portrayal of the area, but scale has however been sacrificed in some cases for the sake of clarity and to fit restrictions of page size.

Walking Close To have taken every care in the research and production of this guide but cannot be held responsible for the safety of anyone using them.

During very wet weather, parts of these walks may become impassable through flooding, check before starting out. Stiles and rights of way can get overgrown during the summer; folding secateurs are a useful addition to a walker's rucksack.

Thanks to Angela for help in production of these booklets

Views or comments?
walkingcloseto@yahoo.co.uk

Walking Close to the Welland
near Stamford

Stamford, from 'Stone Ford', owes its existence to the prehistoric crossing point over the Welland used until the building of the first bridge. More recently it was until the coming of the railways a major coaching stop on the Great North Road between London and York, the coaches requiring two days to travel from London and a further two to reach York. The town's narrow winding streets still carried the substantial north-south traffic of the Great North Road until the completion of the bypass in 1960.

The town retains a great deal of old world charm, Tudor, Stuart and Georgian stone buildings are still grouped around a largely medieval street pattern. There were once 16 churches here. Five older ones and a more modern (Victorian) example survive plus another which has been converted into a series of shops!

Fineshade Abbey (Walk no 5) had been an Augustinian Monastery from the 13th Century until the Reformation. A later Georgian stately home on this site owned by the Monkton family was demolished before the Second World War. An information centre here is useful to those interested in the Red Kite, an exciting bird of prey recently reintroduced into the Rockingham Forest area.

Sir Malcolm Sargent, the conductor famous for his performances in the Proms was born in Stamford in 1895; he died in 1967 and is buried in the town's cemetery. Daniel Lambert, another well known local, was however only visiting Stamford Races when he died in 1809, though only 5ft tall he weighed 53st. A waxwork of him can be seen in the town's museum.

Tolethorpe Hall (Walk no 3) is the location every year for a widely acclaimed season of Shakespearian open air theatrical productions.

The tiny shape of the Long Tailed Tit may be seen in the area; with a tail more than half its length it cannot be mistaken for any other bird. They live in woodland, hedges and scrubby land, in small groups out of the breeding season constantly on the move, flitting from tree to bush or down the length of a hedgerow.

We feel that it would be difficult to get lost with the instructions and map in this booklet, but recommend carrying an Ordnance Survey map. All walks are on Explorer Map No 234, with a small section of walk 10 on map no 247; Landranger Maps Nos. 130, 141 and 142 cover at a smaller scale. Roads, geographical features and buildings, not on our map but visible from the walk can be easily identified.

5:G

1 Wothorpe Groves

5¹/₂ Miles   2¹/₂ Hours

Park in the Bath Row car park in Stamford (pay and display), toilets close by, pubs, restaurants and cafés in town (250yds).

1 Leave the car park by the central footbridge over the stream and turn right, bear right and walk across to the gate by the river, go through and keep parallel with the telegraph poles to the next gate. Turn right past the house, over the bridge and up the slope, after 300yds turn left at the footpath sign on the hedged road between the allotments and cross the stile at the end.

2 Keep direction over the field, a path should be visible through any crop, continue on the right hand side of the left hand field to the cattle grid on the tarmac driveway by the stone wall. Turn left downhill, bear left/ahead on the hardcore track and cross the river on the footbridge at the sluice. farm road. Bear left at the corner then leave the road to go between the farm buildings.

3 Turn right on the grass track with the Welland to the right and go under the bridge at the A1. Carry on all the way to the signpost by the footbridge at Tinwell.

4 Take the field edge to the left with the hedge to the right, go past the fence and into the field; bear right over the field to a white gate.

5 Cross over the railway and carry on up the right hand side of the field, as the hedge stops maintain direction to the hedge corner and bear left with the hedge on the right. Turn right in the corner and continue up this track to Easton-on-the-Hill.

6 At the War Memorial turn left along the High Street. Walk up to the A43; turn left along the path and cross after 150yds. Go along the bridleway signposted to Wothorpe. Keep going Past Wothorpe Groves; turn left along the hardcore farm road just before the imposing but derelict four turreted Wothorpe House.

7 Bear right to a stile, cross to the right hand side of the field past the cottage and through the dip; bear left between the stone building and the stream. Go through the kissing gate and the underpass beneath the A1. Turn right on the other side, up the steps and parallel with the road and go through the gap in the wall.

8 Turn left, follow the left hand field edge bearing left and cross a stile; go over this field on a very slight diagonal, cross a footbridge and continue down a hedged path into a cul-de-sac. At the T-junction go straight over (slight left) and walk down another hedged path, go through the kissing gate at the end and cross to the kissing gate in the opposite corner. Carry on over the ramshackle stile and sleeper footbridge and bear left to the remains of a kissing gate made of upright iron railings; follow the fence to the A43.

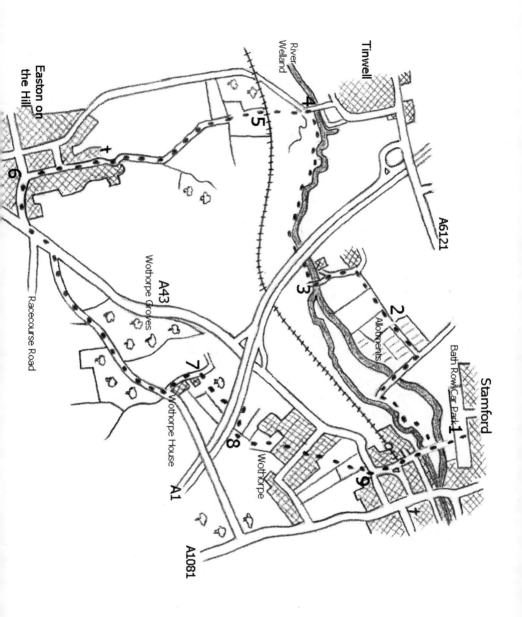

9 Continue ahead, bear left at the fork into Wothorpe Road, walk down the slope, over footbridges across both arms of the Welland to the car park and your vehicle.

2 Fort Henry

6 Miles $2^{1}/_{2}$ Hours

Park in Greetham village, no toilets, local pubs the 'Wheatsheaf', the 'Black Horse' and the 'Plough'. This village is quite small with narrow streets and parking could be a problem, there is no easy alternative.

1 Start from the 'Wheatsheaf'. Take Wheatsheaf Lane, along the back of the pub after 120yds bear left past a marker post, up the field edge with the trees and stream to he left. Carry on to the footbridge and cross.

2 Continue up the slope ahead with the fence to the left and step over the stile at the top. Turn right, up the field edge with the hedge to the right and bear left to the marker post; cross this low piece of fence and turn left along the wide track between the golf course and the hedge. Follow the track left, through a hedge gap and right, with the hedge to the right again. The track continues, bearing right to a marker post, turn left to the brick footpath and follow it right and left.

3 The footpath passes left of the clubhouse and hotel, then continues right of the maintenance building, down the tarmac access road between hedges. At the marker post at the corner of the large pond bear right, then left upslope. Leave the hardcore road, keep straight on to a marker post and bear right, through trees. Carry on left, downslope, passing left of two more large ponds; bear left over the footbridge and right, to the signpost at the top of the embankment.

4 Turn right for 40yds to the signpost and take the steps down, walk along the path parallel to the stream left of Fort Henry and the Lake to the tarmac bridleway.

5 Take the road right, between the lakes and bear right at the fork; continue for just over a mile to where the road forks again and bear right to the stile between tracks at the next fork.

6 Go over, cross the field and the midway dyke to the stile at the corner of the bridleway by the trees. Take the estate road upslope with the trees to the left.

7 As this road swings left at the signpost, turn right along the track to the marker post. Cross the stile/footbridge, go through the gate and up the left hand field edge with the trees to the left. Keep direction on the narrow path and the driveway. As the driveway starts to bear left, carry on ahead along the narrow path to Main Street in Greetham.

Fort Henry was built between 1786-89, named after Henry Noel, 6th Earl of Gainsborough. It was used as a family base for boating activities on the lake, including re-enactments of famous naval battles.

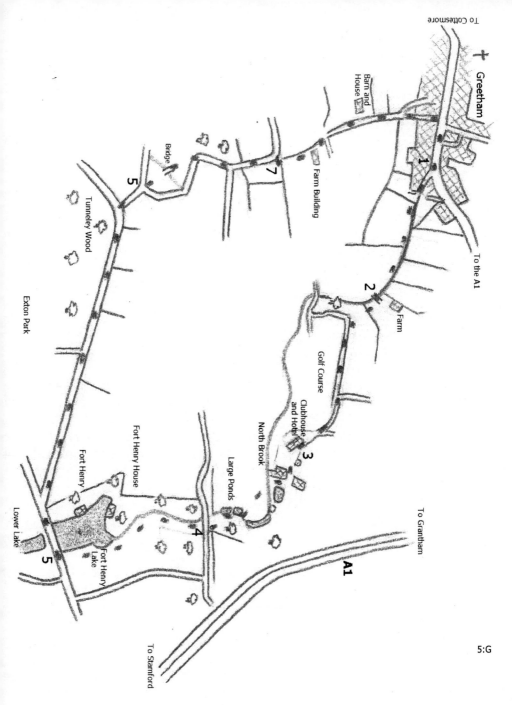

3 Tolethorpe Park

8 Miles $3^3/_4$ Hours

Park in the village of Ryhall, local shop, two local pubs the 'Wicked Witch' and the 'Green Dragon'. No toilets.

1 Start from the village hall, face the library opposite, turn right and walk down the length of The Balk ahead. Cross the main road, go down the slight slope and along the farm road beside the trees. Turn right then left with the road, as it turns right again leave the road and follow the track left/ahead across the field past the telegraph pole to the hedge. Turn left, then right through the hedge and over the stile. Cross the corner of the field, continue direction up the road past Tolethorpe Park and cross the bridge over the River Gwash.

2 Just past the bridge turn right into the field, walk slightly right following the course of the river. Go over two stiles and turn left at the fence, continue uphill to the road. Turn left along the road, past the junction with the road back to Tolethorpe, to a gateway on the right.

3 Go through and walk up the grass bridleway, past the ruined pill box and the inset corner. Continue on this obvious track, with the trees and hedge to the right and a young tree plantation on the left, past a three way signpost, into a dip.

4 Turn right and immediate left through a gate above a stile and carry on upslope to a three way signpost. Bear left, still through trees and cross a stile next to a high wide gate. Keep ahead on the wide left hand field edge, through a wide gap in the boundary to a T-junction with a hardcore farm road.

5 Take the farm road left, with the hedge to the left, to a junction and keep straight on/left, with the hedge now right. As this track swings left take the grassy track ahead between the trees and the hedge. Carry on through the kissing gate to the road.

6 Turn right, go up and then down the slope into Pickworth village; at the junction turn right into The Drift.

7 Walk for nearly a mile and a half along this green lane past the signpost on the right near the houses and onto the tarmac road.

8 As the road swings left, turn right at the sign, over the footbridge and cross the field in the arrowed direction, this field may be under cultivation but a path should be visible, to the left hand corner of the wood. Go over the farm road and continue up the slope, a track should again be well marked within any crop, in the direction of the arrow. Go up the steps and through the gate by the yellow top post. Bear right and walk up the track keeping the farm to the left. Bear left then right at marker posts and continue down the right hand side of the left hand field. Go through the tight hedge gap at the marker post just left of the corner, take a slight left hand diagonal across two stiles and turn left to the B1176 road.

The road between the B1176 and point 3 is now quite busy.

An alternative is to carry on along the road out of Tolethorpe to the junction and turn left along a shorter section of this road.

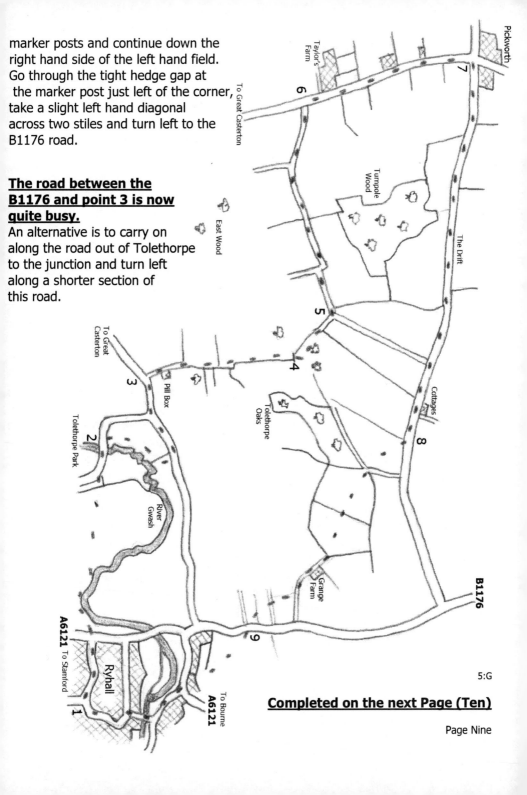

5:G

Completed on the next Page (Ten)

9   Cross the road and continue direction from the gate and signpost to the bottom corner, go through the hedge gap, down the right hand field edge and the enclosed path to the A6121. Turn left and cross the river, back into the village to find your vehicle.

---

4   Easton Hillside

$5^1/_2$ Miles $2^1/_2$ Hours

Park in the Bath Row car park in Stamford (pay and display), other car parks locally if full. Pubs, cafes and shops in the town.

1   Cross the river over the footbridge from the midway point of the car park, walk along the tarmac path and over the next substantial footbridge across the Welland. Keep direction over the crossroads and up the slope of the street ahead (Wothorpe Road). Go over Kettering Road (the A43) at the T-junction.

2   Go straight ahead at the signpost between the hedge and the railings. Continue through the kissing gate, across the field on a right hand diagonal and through the kissing gate in the opposite corner. Turn left, cross the stile, go uphill and over the stile at the top; turn left and walk up to and across the old Great North Road.

3   Continue uphill to the bridleway sign on the right, turn right along this hardcore track, cross the bridge over the dual carriageway and maintain direction past the farm and through the trees to the A43. Go over the road and turn left.

4   Turn immediate right into Easton on the Hill along the High Street. Take the second right down West Street, follow as it bears left then go right at the fork, signed Byway. Continue downhill over the railway, keep direction along the grass path and walk up to the concrete bridge with iron railings.

5   Do not cross, turn right and walk along the bank with the River Welland on the left. Carry on under the Great North Road, turn left after a quarter of a mile over a footbridge, turn right on the other side back to the original direction but take the path that veers away from the river towards the church spires of Stamford. Keep to the right of the telegraph poles at a fork. The path runs closer to the river again past Roman Ford, carry on to the tarmac path between the footbridges traversed earlier; turn left back to the car park and your vehicle.

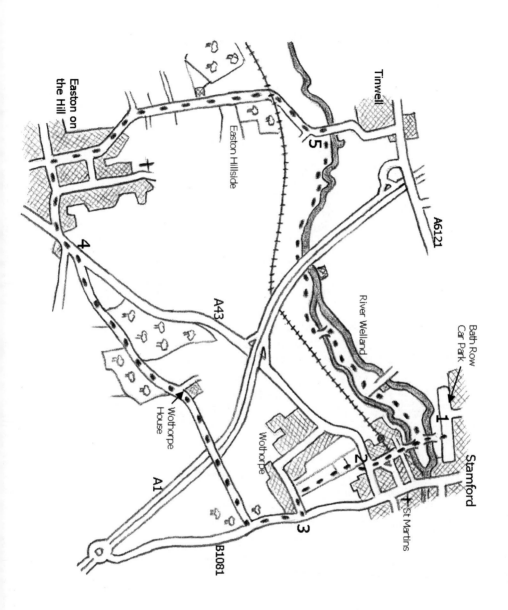

5   Fineshade Abbey

9³/₄ Miles   4¹/₂ Hours

Park in the Wakerley Great Wood car park,
between Wakerley and the A43, toilets and picnic facilities.

1   Leave on the hardcore Bridleway past the green barrier
at the entrance. As this track swings right turn left at
a marker post, after 100yds turn right at another
marker post. At the bottom of a slope turn right a
short distance, then left at a marker post, upslope
again. Keep direction out of the trees, over a stile,
across the next field and over the stile in the tree
line. Take a slight diagonal to a gate, turn left
and walk up to the A43.

2   Cross and continue direction over this field and
the concrete bridge at the corner of the trees. Turn left
and follow the arrowed direction uphill past the marker
post and along the path between wire fences; bear left after
the stile and then right at a marker post. Cross the stile
and maintain direction on the path through the trees and
over the next field to the road, this field may be under
cultivation but a track should be visible within any crop.

3   Turn right over the old railway bridge, bear right on the
road past the buildings and right again onto the stony
bridleway; follow as it swings right then left and keep going as it
enters Westhay Wood. Carry on at a T-junction on a less
substantial track, past a metal gate to the signpost.

4   Turn left, passing left of the sawmill and keep direction with the
fence to the right; after half a mile join the forest road
ahead/right. Be very careful here! The road swings left 100yds after
a Jurassic Way marker post; take the lesser track straight on, confirmed after 50yds
by another Jurassic Way marker. Enter and keep direction through Fineshade
Wood, the track leads eventually on a well defined path to the A43.

5   Turn right along the roadside path and bear left along High Street past the
'Royal Oak' into Duddington. Turn left into Mill Street walk down to the bridge and
cross over the Welland. Continue straight on (the Jurassic Way goes right here) and
bear left on the tarmac path next to the old route of the A47.

A47

6

Welland Spinney

Tixover

River Welland

Duddington

5:G

5

A43

†

Fineshade Wood

Caravan Site

Take Care Here!

3

Red Kite Centre

Westhay Wood

Sawmill

Fineshade Abbey

2

4

6 Turn left through Tixover village; keep direction at the end through the gateway and along the farm road past a yellow topped Marker post. Carry on bearing right, past a yellow top post at a metal gate, along the left hand field edge through another gate to the corner and turn right to a narrow gate at a yellow top marker post. Follow the track through Welland Spinney and out through the gate.

Completed on the next page (Fourteen)

Completion of 5 Fineshade Abbey

7   Continue on the left hand field edge above the river, through a field boundary to a hedge gap with yellow top posts either side and follow the right hand edge of this field with the hedge to the right up to the road. Turn left along the road over the river into Wakerley and left again at the T-junction.

8   Turn immediate right up the footpath at the top left of the gravel drive, bear left from the stile across the field to the next stile and continue on the left hand field edge. At the corner of the churchyard turn left and follow the edge of the field to the road at the signpost. Turn right along the road and go around the double bend. Turn right at the almost hidden Jurassic Way marker post into Wakerley Great Wood; bear left to join a track to the car park and your vehicle.

---

6   Pit Lane

4 Miles   2 Hours

Park in Ketton village, no toilets, local pubs and shop. Start form the western end of the village at the cross roads of High Street, Luffenham Road, Church Road and Empingham Road.

1   Walk a few steps along Empingham Road and turn right at the footpath sign on the concrete path next to the cottage. Turn left down the gravel and tarmac road; turn right at Manor Green and keep direction between the wall and the fence, past the cycle barriers and carry on between walls. Turn left at the footpath sign and follow the hedge right, then left in the corner by the metal gate. Turn right and left again at the next corners and follow the hedge to a stile next to a yellow top post.

2   Cross and join the hardcore farm road running left; continue uphill past the cattle grid to a stile and a yellow top marker post on the right. Follow the arrowed direction across the field which may be under cultivation a path however should be visible through any crop; to a kissing gate in the trees ahead.

3   Go through the gate and bear left through the trees, turn right after 150yds to a T-junction and follow the wide track right. continue with the wire fence and factory buildings to the right and go through the kissing gate at the end.

4   Bear slightly right onto the tarmac Pit Lane and go down past the roundabout to the A6121, turn left and walk up to the footpath sign opposite the cement works entrance and turn right.

5 Go down the track and keep straight on across the bridge over the river Chater, turn left and go through the gate, bear right on the stony track uphill and turn left in the corner keeping the hedge to the right. Continue direction, bearing slightly right and go under the railway arch.

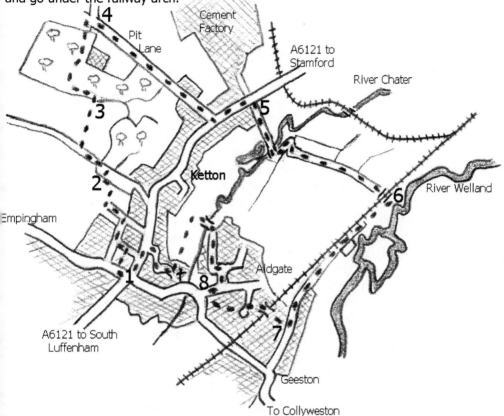

6 Turn right, walk parallel to the railway and over the stile, continue down the narrow path between the fence and the railway. Bear left between the houses to a signpost for the Hereward Way.

7 Turn right and follow the path as it bears right at the fence corner and crosses the railway by a footbridge. Walk between fences and cross the road, through the kissing gate and the next gate, down the slope, through the wide gateway to the signpost and turn right, along the road.

8 Carry on bearing left past a half-timbered house, turn left at a T-junction (marker disc on telegraph pole), bear right and walk up to the footbridge and cross back over the Chater. Turn left at the footpath sign over the second footbridge and cross the field to the end at the right of the play equipment. Walk past the end of the cottage and follow the stony road to the right uphill to the High Street. Turn left the short distance to the crossroads.

7 Tickencote Park

$6^1/_2$ Miles   3 Hours

Park in Great Casterton, no toilets, pubs the 'Plough' and the 'Crown' and the OK Diner snack bar where the A1081 slip road joins the Great North Road.

1   Start from the crossroads; take the road to Ingthorpe, go across the bridge over the A1 and turn right at the bridleway sign into the farmyard. Follow the track left through the gate and continue past the house with the low stone wall to the right.

2   Bear left at the marker post to a hedge gap keeping to the right of the telegraph pole over a field which may be under cultivation, the track however should be visible within any crop. Continue over the field to the next hedge gap and take a left hand diagonal; maintain direction over the next three fields marked by yellow topped posts. Turn slight left to the yellow top marker post at the road.

3   Turn right along the side of the A606; as the road starts to rise out of the dip cross the stile to the right and take a shallow diagonal left moving gradually away from the road. Cross the stile close to the trees and the next, just ahead. Follow the edge of the field trees on the right to the marker post then continue over the field to the next stile. Cross both stiles at the field entrance, go along the left hand field edge and keep direction when the fence stops. Maintain direction through a hedge gap and cross the double stile at the corner of four fields, carry on to the stile ahead, cross and turn right.

4   Go down the field edge and cross the footbridge, bear right to the marker post at the corner of the cottage. Turn left and keep along this road to the T-junction.

5   Turn right for 150yds and then bear right up the bridleway between trees; continue along the field edge, join a concrete farm road and keep direction, approaching Chapel Field Spinney with the hedge on the left. Keep to the left through the spinney and continue ahead between hedges and along the field edge.

6   From the marker post cross to the opposite corner, the track should be visible within any crop. Join the farm road straight on between hedge and saplings, at the T-junction turn right then cross the stile to the left. Go over the field diagonally to the yellow topped post to the right of the cottages and join the tarmac road left.

7   As this road swings left, go straight on down the right hand side of the field. Cross the stile into Tickencote Park and take a gentle curve right to the yellow topped post at the fence; continue over the drive and the next piece of parkland and go out onto the road in Tickencote village. Turn right through the village; go straight on through the gate at the end, across the field and over the stile.

8   Turn right and follow this slip road under the Great North road, back into the village of Great Casterton and your vehicle.

The route will be very
muddy when wet

5:G

Page Seventeen

8 Shillingthorpe Park

$6^1/_2$ Miles $2^3/_4$ Hours

Find a parking space in Braceborough, No facilities.

1 Start from the High Street. Turn left (west) at the footpath sign, up the path right of the garden between the fence and the hedge. Cross the footbridge and bear left over the field which may be under cultivation although a track should be well marked through any crop. Go past the end of the trees and turn left, in front of the house.

2 Turn immediate right at the marker post, with the house to the right. Cross the field to the left of the telegraph pole, carry on through the hedge gap and take a left hand diagonal over the field (which should have a track through any crop) to the signpost in the opposite corner next to the road and the farm. Turn right on the road for 700yds to the bridleway sign on the left.

3 Turn left and follow the track between fields as it veers left then right, go past the wood; cross a field boundary and continue on the left hand field edge with the pylons to the left as it meanders over the bridge across the railway, over the footbridge next to the ford and on to the road.

4 Take the road left, over the level crossing and walk for just over half a mile. Go through the kissing gate on the left next to the footpath signpost and follow the stony tree lined drive. Swing right then left over the West Glen River and maintain direction on the track through the park, go through the gate and up the wide track through the trees up to the footpath signpost on the right.

5 Turn right, cross through a kissing gate and bear right through the next; cross the field ahead (a track should be visible within any crop). At the boundary bear right continuing on a track over this field to the bottom right corner, go through the boundary and follow the field edge to the corner.

6 Take the path left between the fence and the conifers. Turn right over a footbridge along the right hand edge of a garden with a concrete fence to the right; go left down the gravel drive to the road.

7 Turn left along the road, as it swings left go straight on down the track between fields, turn right at the marker post in the corner and then left over the footbridge. Cross the field ahead, keep direction over two more stiles and go through the gate. Continue along the road and bear left into the village to find your vehicle.

Shillingthorpe Hall was built in 1833 and used as a mental hospital by John Willi the son of Robert; the hall was demolished in 1949.

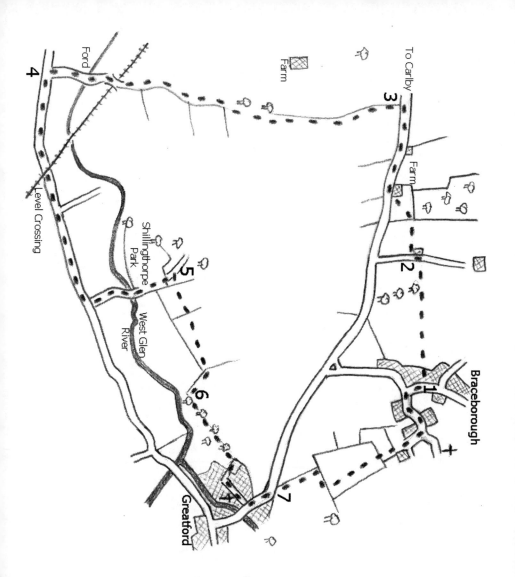

The first Greatford Hall was built in the 16th century; it was used as a private hospital for the treatment of mental illness by Robert Willis (1718-1807). His most famous patient was King George III who probably came here during his battle with porphyria during the latter part of his reign. The hall burnt down in 1922 and was rebuilt in much the same style as the original. It was occupied towards the end of the last century by Harry Dowsett who founded the local concrete company Dow-Mac. Note the concrete fence! It is a private residence.

5:G

9 Tinwell Crossing

9¹/₄ Miles

4¹/₂ Hours

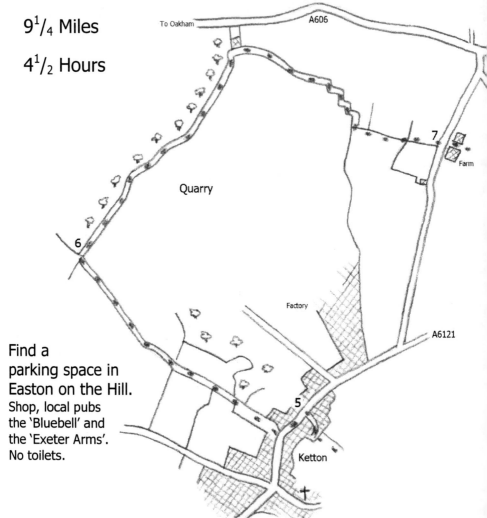

To Oakham

A606

7

Farm

Quarry

6

Factory

A6121

Find a
parking space in
Easton on the Hill.
Shop, local pubs
the 'Bluebell' and
the 'Exeter Arms'.
No toilets.

5

Ketton

1 From the war memorial go down the High Street past the 'Bluebell', go straight on at the crossroads along Westfields past the Post Office and continue down the tarmac bridleway called Ketton Drift. As the drift ends at a gate bear left over a stile and take the arrowed direction over the field ahead, this field and others in this way may be under cultivation but a track should be visible through any crops. Keep direction through hedge gaps and past yellow topped marker posts to the road.

2 Turn right along the road, over the Welland and on to the Ketton sign, follow the bend right and go straight on into Geeston.

3 Turn left along the footpath signposted Aldgate, bear right at the fence corner and cross the railway on the footbridge. Walk between hedges across the road marked by yellow topped posts, go through the kissing gate and the next gate, down the slope, through the wide gateway and turn right by the signpost.

4 Bear left past a half timbered house, turn left at the T-junction, bear right and walk up to a footbridge and cross over the River Chater. Follow the path ahead, turn right past the front of the chapel and then left up Bull Lane.

5 Turn left along the High Street to the footpath sign at Home Farm and turn right; go through the farmyard and turn left through the gate at the signpost close to the Dutch barns.

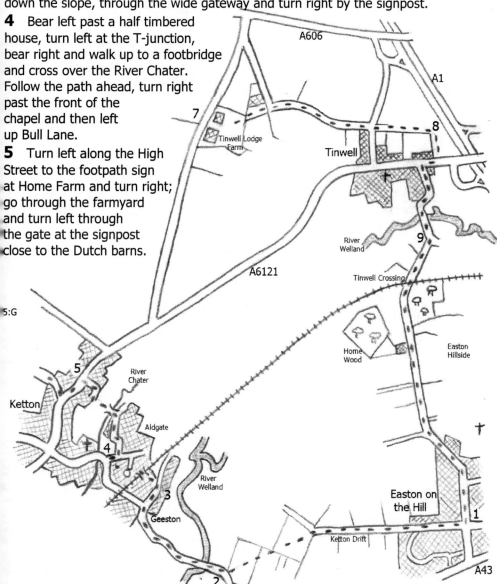

Walk up the slope on this hardcore farm road, bear right at a junction, go past a barn and continue to a wind pump. Keep along this path to the gate at the end.

Completed on the next page (Twenty Two)

6   Turn right along the track between the trees and the quarry to the end, follow the path right and keep going on this obvious track around several corners. Turn left over a stile and carry on along the left hand edge of this field, go over a stile and walk up to the road.

7   Cross the road and keep straight on along the concrete surface between the barns and downslope on the wide double track, left of the power line pole. Step over the stile at the next pole and the stile at the yellow top marker post, by the wooden gate. Keep direction over the stile at the signpost ahead. Continue straight on down the narrow tarmac road to the T-junction and cross the stile ahead. Carry on down the right hand field edge to the marker post at the corner.

8   Turn right, down to the road and right to Mill Lane. Take this road left, at the bottom go past the first footpath sign and bear left at the next bridleway sign; follow the path to the right at the river and cross the bridge to the left.

9   Keep direction with the hedge to the right, then bear right along a hedge lined path up to the railway at Tinwell Crossing. Go over and follow this byway all the way into Easton on the Hill and your vehicle.

---

10   Pickworth Great Wood

5 Miles   2$\frac{1}{2}$ Hours

Find a parking space in Pickworth, there is sometimes room on the wide untended verges of the road towards the A1. No facilities.

1   Start from the church and take the road towards the A1. Turn right at the signpost just before the derestriction signs and walk up the hardcore farm road between fences past Lodge Farm. Bear left at the marker post over the field in the arrowed direction to the hedge corner and follow the field edge with the hedge and the dyke to the left all the way to the trees.

2   Continue ahead on the track through between Pickworth Great Wood and Holywell Wood, keep direction on the more substantial track. Carry on as the trees on the left end bearing right downhill to the road.

3   Cross the road and take the left hand footpath ahead; just past the house turn left on the hardcore farm road. Go through the gate, bear right and follow the road. At the end go straight on past two marker posts over the field ahead, this field may be under cultivation but a path should be visible within any crop.

4   Pass through the gates, go straight on over the T-junction into Clipsham and follow the road left. As the road starts to swing right, turn left at the Bridleway signpost; go through the gate and bear left through the second gate. Bear right on the grass path between fences and continue past White's Plantation.

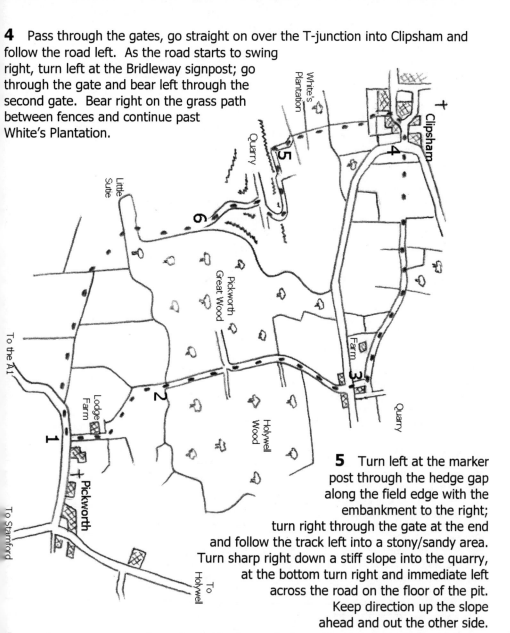

5   Turn left at the marker post through the hedge gap along the field edge with the embankment to the right; turn right through the gate at the end and follow the track left into a stony/sandy area. Turn sharp right down a stiff slope into the quarry, at the bottom turn right and immediate left across the road on the floor of the pit. Keep direction up the slope ahead and out the other side.

5   At the top continue along the field edge with the trees of Pickworth Great Wood to the left. Cross over the footbridge (right of the corner); go through the spur of trees called Little Sutie and bear left across the corner of the field. Pass through the concrete gateposts and carry on along the farm track with the hedge to the left up to the road. Turn left back into Pickworth village to find your vehicle.

The 'Walking Close to' Series

South and South West

Salisbury and Stonehenge
The New Forest (North and West)
Romsey and the Test Valley
Cheddar Gorge
Exmouth and East Devon
Corsham and Box (Wiltshire)
The Quantock Hills (West Somerset)
Blandford Forum (Dorset)
Chichester and the South Downs

Winchester and the South Downs
The New Forest (South and East)
The East Devon Coast
Glastonbury and the City of Wells
The Avon near Bath
The Avon near Chippenham (Wiltshire)
Shaftesbury (Dorset)
Bradford-on-Avon (Wiltshire)

East Anglia and Lincolnshire

The Nene near Peterborough
Lavenham (Suffolk)
The Nene Valley Railway near Wansford
The Nene near Oundle
The Great North Road near Stilton
Bury St Edmunds
Norfolk Broads (Northern Area)
Southwold and the Suffolk Coast
North West Norfolk (Hunstanton and Wells)
North Norfolk (Cromer and Sheringham)
The Lincolnshire Wolds (North)
The Stour near Sudbury (Suffolk)
Chelmsford
Epping Forest (Essex/North London)
The Colne near Colchester
Thetford Forest (Norfolk/Suffolk)
The Great Ouse in Huntingdonshire
The Torpel Way (Stamford to Peterborough)

Grafham Water (Huntingdonshire)
Dedham Vale (Suffolk/Essex)
The Cam and the Granta near Cambridge
Lincoln
The Welland near Stamford
The Isle of Ely
Norfolk Broads (Southern Area)
Aldeburgh, Snape and Thorpeness
Clare, Cavendish and Haverhill
Bourne and the Deepings
The Lincolnshire Wolds (South)
The Orwell near Ipswich
Stowmarket (Suffolk)
Hertford and the Lee Valley
Newmarket
The Great Ouse near King's Lynn
South Lincolnshire

Midlands

The Nene near Thrapston
The Nene near Wellingborough
The River Ise near Kettering
The Nene near Northampton
Rockingham Forest (Northamptonshire)
Daventry and North West Northamptonshire
Rugby
Stratford-upon-Avon
Rutland Water
Eye Brook near Uppingham
The Soar near Leicester
Lutterworth (Leicestershire)
The Vale of Belvoir (North Leicestershire)
Melton Mowbray
The Welland near Market Harborough
Banbury
South West Herefordshire

The Great Ouse near Bedford
Woburn Abbey (Bedfordshire)
Sherwood Forest
Pitsford Water (Northamptonshire)
The Thames near Oxford
The Trent near Nottingham
The Vale of White Horse
Henley-on-Thames
The River Pang (Reading/Newbury)
The Great Ouse north of Milton Keynes
The Cotswolds near Witney
The Malvern Hills
The Dukeries (Sherwood Forest)
The Severn near Worcester
Woodstock and Blenheim Palace
The Kennet near Newbury

Cumbria

Cartmel and Southern Lakeland